PERSEPHONE
IN THE LATE ANTHROPOCENE

PERSEPHONE
IN THE LATE ANTHROPOCENE

poems

MEGAN GRUMBLING

ACRE

CINCINNATI 2020

Acre Books is made possible by the support of the Robert and Adele Schiff Foundation and the Department of English at the University of Cincinnati.

Designed by Barbara Neely Bourgoyne
Cover art: Justin Francavilla, "Reflection," ink on paper, 24 in. x 32 in.

ISBN-13 (pbk) 978-1-946724-32-8
ISBN-13 (ebook) 978-1-946724-33-5

The press is based at the University of Cincinnati, Department of English, McMicken Hall, Room 248, PO Box 210069, Cincinnati, OH, 45221–0069.

Acre Books books may be purchased at a discount for educational use. For information please email business@acre-books.com.

for Denis

CONTENTS

II. SEARCH

III. DESCENT

IV. AND ASCENT

Persephone in the Late Anthropocene began its life as an experimental spoken opera, cocreated by me as librettist and the late Denis Nye as composer, and it was developed through the work of many artists and performers over the years of 2014–16. The full-length opera premiered in May 2016, as a Hinge/Works production staged at SPACE Gallery, in Portland, Maine.

This book is an expansion of the opera's original libretto. I encourage readers to listen to recordings of the beautiful scores that have inspired and accompanied these words, at www.hingeworks.org/persephone-in-the-late-anthropocene.

I. ASCENT

She Was Pulling

(Mother's Song)

What happened was, she was pulling
at something. A flower?

Yes, maybe. Narcissus
it might have been.

Her tendons sprung shadows
as she gripped, as the flower tripped

a spasm seizing all
the way below.

And when its root gave way,
what happened was

her going below, cold
and swallow.

Everyone knows
that part.

While She Was Gone

What happened was, while she was gone
and I disguised by grief and rags,

limping through blight and briar
for a glimpse of her light,

some people were kind,
drew my sack-clad bones

to table and fire, filled bowls.
One blathered herself blue

to make me smile. So I gave them a plough.
Seeds. And mysteries. Not everyone knows

that part. Mysteries? Mysteries
are, well, not secrets

exactly. Anyone could learn them. Let's say
they were a story. Or a cup. Let's say

they were some part mirror
some part scythe.

A Different Kind of Pulling

What happened was, much later, a different kind of pulling.
A string for a bell, sweets from a bowl, sheets

from a bed. This pulling was much easier
than with that tough root. And she went on and on,

dingdingding, syrup, and silk
all day long. A taste for more

than mysteries. Mysteries? Mysteries
are misunderstood now. A mystery

isn't an unknown.
You are growing one right now in your throat.

Which is louder, cold or heat?

seeing her together
(the Chorus)

We'd all had sightings, the odd ghost of her gold or green in otherwise cold. But we were always alone, always chalked it up to our own visions or intoxications. Our desire. Our paranoia. Now we were seeing her together, crowding close to watch her suck an ice cube small or lose a stocking in the surf. That was when things began to change. The mood. Something about our mouths. The way we spoke her name, swallowed all we could see to swill.

short shorts

At first, it was all biergartens and orange Dreamsicles. She wasn't supposed to be around now—these were her months to be away with him, eating stones and stroking clocks. Or whatever she did with him. But she had chosen *us*. And at first it was all holiday, all innocent debauchery whenever she appeared out of season: Here she was in a canary-yellow halter dress, opening flows of hoppy ale. Here she was in short shorts, drenching us in dandelion fizz, or with huge buttercups, grazing our chins with yolk-gold. We made merry, made noise, made hay, made out like magpies. Then she was gone again. She left us each time with our suddenly bared skin, our yellowed chins, and our chosenness, with our schoolchild sensation of having gotten away with something slight but delicious.

The New Farmer's Almanac Folklore for January

Avoid whistling in doorways, as you may wake the Rains.

The New Farmer's Almanac Word of the Day

An *exaltation* is a flock of larks.

Persephone's Lark Song

I go for the light, the light, a love
of heights and thaw. Sweets out of season.
Daylong trilling *trrly* and *prrit*.
A whole flock's skyward veer and the white
of underwing.

Living in the dark takes will. Irony.
A strong stomach for dearth, dearth, dried fruit.
And no harm, time to time, to sing too much
in the sun, exotic plums, fresh blistered lemon
on the lips.

These flights are just a lark, a lark, a least
creature's thirst quenched. I do descend, in time.
Once I've soared trilling out of sight,
I'll fold back wings and fall
like a stone.

From *"Man on Man"*:
A New Popular Anthropology of the Anthropocene

I.2 Myth and Ritual

i.   In her earliest incarnations, Persephone descended to Hades by way of abduction. By the early Anthropocene, however, the impetus of her descent was more frequently told as seduction or, later, outright will, in the idioms of self-discovery, independence, and even, for a time, revolt.

. . .

iv.   Ancient pre-Anthropocenean rituals celebrated a progression of rites, of which one phase—a reenactment of the original Persephone story—was known as the *dromena*, or the "things done." These ritual phases began with "Descent," representing Persephone's abduction; moved on to "Search," during which time Demeter pursued her daughter; and concluded with Persephone's "Ascent" back aboveground—a resolution that devotees are thought to have observed in the drinking of a hallucinatory grog.

In the early Anthropocene, the "Ascent" phase came to be celebrated with greater frequency and scale, albeit via less formalized ceremonies and with a shift in the ritual: participants now imbibed less in celebration of fertility than in protest of its insufficiency.

trying so hard

It was when she moved into the gazebo that things got strained. There she was for a week at a time, clenching blood oranges into terra-cotta, crushing thyme with the butt of a trowel. Smiling and trying so hard. The desperate screech of her tools against the clay. We were no longer surprised to see her. Pitied her, even. And it was for that, now, that we stripped and lay down with her in snow and snowmelt, and that we came up dripping, each time, our elbows and hip bones both bloodied and rinsed by rotting ice.

Blues Song

The blues, down there, got dark.
Slate-blue, bruised cobalt. Worse than the usual
solemnities, the chilled goblet and robe.
Nightshade and coal. Cold sentences
of *cannot*,

The blues leave blind spots.
Somewhere between the blue of need
and the blue of want, my eyes cease
to adjust. To abide my milk-blue cast
in the glass.

The blues send me above for a dose
of solace, robin's egg and gold.
Summer freckles, honey and rose.
This town's ever warmer harbor
nearly green.

The blues beg bright things freed.
Beg larkspur in my brow, lemon
in my blonde. Inklings far too fair
and far too fleet to be kept
in the dark.

her lover

She had taken a lover here. One of us. That was the latest. She couldn't stay away, couldn't say no. Peeled him grapes, carved them into rosebuds and tiny, big-bosomed nymphs, floated them in bowls of pennyroyal, egg white and rye. Indulged his slightest whim—peach-sweet strawberries, apples crossed with Concord grapes. Contorted limbs and throat to fit his kiss. This lover was a reckless inebriate, it was said. A narcissist. Partial to unnatural rituals. One of us, it was said. We were stricken at the thought. But stirred. Jealous, and thus ravenous.

Adultery Song

Sugar enhanced, supersweet, all
I can eat. Our butter and sheen
are boundless, blood-engorged, our appetites
audacious, a drunken just-once thrust
every dawn.

We feast on savoy spliced with scorpions,
tomatoes that taste of rose. Rut our thumbs
in bowls of writhing elvers still alive. Bend rivers and seas
to the whims of our bed. Milk spider-silk
for our sheets.

So I slant-lie, shill the calendar
with alibis, the extra equinox. The only true
betrayal is to cheat oneself. Abundance
is our birthright, and the only sin on earth
to abstain.

The New Farmer's Almanac Migration Forecast

Larks, starlings, and swallows south of the Maritimes are expected to again winter in place. In some songbirds, Desynchronized Migratory Restlessness Disorders may result in heightened risk to livestock, jetports, and plate glass.

thirsting so hard

Schlitz all morning, sangria all afternoon. It was too hot to work, or else too cold, so we drank with her. The most homage we could muster anymore. It was too hot for lust, let alone for love. Or else too cold. And what a weird mood she set, wetting us down with halved lemons, rubbing our faces with her ten fingers each sunk into an olive. There were more lemons, more olives than anyone knew what to do with. Then, just as suddenly, none, and only brackish water to drink. We were eating so much tapenade, drinking so many shandies—then thirsting so hard—that we began to feel queasily cured from within.

Swallow Song

So long their thousand serif wings
trailed my to and fro. Every equinox
in concert. Each dawn, we rose singing.
Each night, settled like dark leaves
into sleep.

Too often now I come and go
alone. A swallow's wings cannot keep pace
with whim, and too often I've cried
Spring, set them aswerve,
asunder.

For a time, I gorged hard
on pomegranate. God, the heartburn.
Now, husk sucked and gums rinsed red,
I can't get it down. Seeds clog my mouth
like lost teeth.

So many seeds circling
this tongue. A murmuration
of seeds. An exaltation, a murder. A mouth
swarming with larks, with crows,
with swallows.

Some call a flock of swallows
a *gulp*. My own throat
is caught. Won't. Cheeks gravelly
with seed, I garble the songs,
drool a bit.

I'd love those birds to trail me again.
The first swallows spiraled so deep.
Were my very shadow. But I choke
on. Keep faith, keep flocks
from my throat.

From *Cli-Fi and One-Offs: The Anthropocene as Text*

Early in the period came the ascension of the popular literary and cinematic genre of "cli-fi," that is, speculative narratives involving climate change, and, soon thereafter, its cousin: "food-fi." Early iterations of food-fi grew out of the lavishly epicurean style known derisively, in some circles, as "food porn" (perhaps most trenchant as critique of the genre was Wright's parody *Rape of the Lox: Sockeye. Crème Fraîche. Fennel Pollen. Microbeads.*) and later developed into several iterations of a more dystopian-minded speculative genre.

Works of food-fi included fantasies (and, later, satires) of newly created foods (lemons engineered with bioluminescence; "Pat-Protek" seeds, whose second-generation seeds were designed to self-destruct; the much-memed corn strain spliced with quail DNA, ears of which ripened a tiny yolk within each kernel) and the hormonal and neurological consequences of their consumption. Other narratives involved challenges to the successful harvest, transport, or emergency decontamination of a population's food source; mysteries and conspiracy-driven thrillers hinging on mass food-borne mortalities or morbidities; and procedurals depicting detection of nonnormative behavior in bees, butterflies, and songbirds.

her mother

Her mother, of course, had long since been put in the home. Numb to her daughter's sprees. Or else enraged. She was heavily medicated, of course. But it was for her own health. For the greater good. Her clinicians may have fumbled a dosage or played a little loosely with the samples, with the pinkest pills, but we were sure they knew what they were doing. A putty-colored room, a watercolor print of cornucopias.

Winter Feast Song

I went such long winters in want
of pea shoot, corn furl. Now I gorge.
Torpor, tumor. Pods and ears
by the trough.

Lately I long only to feast
on bowls of stones, spoons of light. I starve
for dark. For starving. Our revels now
are endless.

At picnics I can taste dwarf lumps and cleft
tassels in the Xtra Sweet. Dopamine.
Cobalt and ultraviolet.
The split atoms

that shriveled and sugar-cured the seed.
My mother's meals turn shame into starch.
Each raw ear leaks a milk so sweet
it scours.

Atrazine

What happened was antibiotics. Later. Neonicotinoids
and corncorncorn. My atrazine fog.

What happened was no sleep. Endless bedsores and beeping
in these disinfected rooms. She is somewhere

in between, now. I roll the seeds.
Rub my hands in the red. I tell

fortunes: A revolution, a science, a factory.
Dingdingding. I don't tell

the mystery.
I am not to touch

anything. I am not to be touched
without gloves.

The New Farmer's Almanac Home Remedies

Mood swings and rattled nerves are common during extreme
weather events and false seasons. Soothe yourself with compresses
of Saint-John's-wort, or swallow three drops of a tonic of
pennyroyal bitters and rue.

Cleft Song

Some odd solace this hole in the earth
holds. Hours here I crouch, cleave, curve limbs
among root, worm, mycelium.
Graze my eyelashes in the loam
at the lip.

A hiding place, now. A sanctum. This cusp
that I have raced and caught seams to cross,
that I have brushed past, bruised smooth
by my passage—hands, leverage, hems—
I now haunt.

Eyes level with the lip, vision split
between light and loam, I imagine myself
limbless. Imagine myself severed
of might. Mint, crocus, corn sprouting
from my scalp.

revirginize

She had started telling some of us, sober and in all sincerity, that she had found a way to revirginize herself. We doubted it, we knew better. So although we found ourselves following her recipes anyway, rinsing our own sheets in rosewater or charcoal slurry, we couldn't be sure whether we rinsed out of sympathy, dread, or just some kind of crude magical thinking.

II. SEARCH

World of Explaining

What happened was
What happened? The search was on

for why everything was going wrong.
For the cup, for the story. For whodunit.

I was looking for my child underground.
Someone had seen her

slipping through the hole
with red hands and a husk

but she was gone.
Back above, I listened to the people near the hole

tell whodunit. Tell who had

committed allowed hurt killed forgotten chopped soiled

Why she had

lost swallowed renounced splurged given in put out

Why the poor, the dark, and the honeybees were

wasting away drinking the urine thirsting so hard

What happened was there were a lot of ideas.
A lot of suspects. Maybe the revolutionary

was whodunit. Or the scientist. The factory owner.
Dingdingding. And *Mother,*

I knew somewhere my child
was moaning. Choking

on what's-done and what-to-do, so many
hard seeds. Everyone was sick with seeking

whodunit. Seeking to turn the mirror,
solve the scythe.

Suddenly there was a world
of explaining to do.

too susceptible

It was her own fault, that everything was going wrong. The acid and inundation.
The blackouts, the drunken bees, so many green crabs that we raced them in
the street. It was her fundamentally erratic personality. Her wildness, which,
however attractive, was more than a little inconvenient. Dangerous, even.
Anyone who said otherwise was a romantic, a sucker for the most maudlin
kind of sentimentality. For bucolics. Bodice rippers. Others said she was too
fragile, too susceptible—too partial, even—to domination. Some said it was
our duty. Our chosenness, our charity. Her torpor, her pallor, her choking. The
stories went that she binged, that she fasted. That her husband had grown wise.
We debated. Held back the harbor with sand. Swallowed pills. Some crazy old
lady kept setting up a joke, two kids and a pile of rat shit. We bet dimes on our
favorites in the green crab races, but they all looked the same when they lost.

The New Farmer's Almanac Puzzle of the Day

When is a spade like a sieve?

The New Farmer's Almanac Word of the Day

A flock of swallows is called a *gulp*.

The New Farmer's Almanac Good Day

Today is a good day to sharpen blades, clean bottles, or pay debts.

Once Song

Once song went
Rain and conceive
as mysteries were drunk,
Things Done. *Rain and conceive*
was what they called, not just called but sang
in pour and praise,
was what they sang in prayer
and perfect fifths.

Once song went
wrong—just once
I swore, was all I'd spit his dark
seed out, not just spit but gag, rinse
with peroxide and lime. That I'd leave
my mother in the dun and doorless
rooms for days, while I helped the drunks
butcher the chorus.

Once song went
they were already drinking
a rougher grog than mystery. Raising voices
in boredom, riven verse, not just riven but wrung,
wrong. Could their chorus still be sung
in time or unison? Could it even still be called
a song?

From *"Man on Man"*:
A New Popular Anthropology of the Anthropocene

III.2 Food Practices

"Paleo"- and "Hunter/Gatherer"-themed restaurants and diets had long been in ascendance in "foodie" and wellness-conscious circles, and the trend now entered mainstream supermarkets; even some processed foods bore "Paleo-Safe" labels on their packaging.

Meanwhile, the rarified foodie culture turned to ever more minimalist innovations. The renowned chef of Stockholm's Soma began crafting variations on an actual stone soup, using a proprietary "gastro-alchemical" process to extract digestible nutrients from lava stone and beach sand.

Other chefs and restaurateurs co-opted the art world's increasing affinity for non-verbal culture. In some restaurants—Berlin's Istig, Portland's Here—occasional talk-free events, galvanized for diners by so-called "de-consumption artists," evolved to a *raison d'être*: these proprietors eventually replaced restaurant names with symbols, did away with menus entirely, and maintained strict silence in dining rooms, with no sounds permitted but hums, grunts, and clicks.

trouble eating

Or maybe it was her mother's fault. The fire ants. Our flooded beds and swollen tongues. The storm surges and farmers' self-harm. Her mother was to blame for the vandalism. For the unspeakable things left in the river. In the reservoir. Her daughter, meanwhile, stared at us from doorways and the mouths of manholes, curled into the fetal position, slicked her eyelids yellow with yolk. There were bizarre stories, murdered trees. Cannibalism. Genital mutations in frogs, in small mammals. In larger mammals. We were having trouble eating. Acid reflux. Anxious sphincter syndrome. *"Those are smart pills," one kid says to the other*, went the joke. At meals we wore dark glasses or, over our mouths, small napkin-masks, like the ones worn by those who eat songbirds.

Hungry, the Owner

What happened? Maybe someone's ax
made my oak moan. And that was whodunit.

I was looking for my child in the woods.
Someone had seen her curling up

in a hollow spruce, wasp nest,
broken robin's egg.

But she had gone again.
So I walked on, listening to the people tell whodunit:

how what happened was a woman
ate a fruit

that was against the rules. Or someone
ate it, anyway. Most people

have heard that part. Or maybe,
some said, it was because

someone they call John Barleycorn
got buried alive,

got ground under stones. Or
how the someone with the ax

a farmer father builder banker soldier owner drunkard priest

who'd had a taste

for blood firewood vandalism a table a murder a garden a bed had made my oak bleed.

How so maybe I made him hungry, the owner
of the ax. So hungry that the more he ate

the hungrier he got. Not everyone knows
that part either.

How I made the owner of the ax
so hungry that he gnawed

on his own knuckles. Gnawed
on the lean pillow of meat between

his thumb
and his finger. And *Mother*,

somewhere my child was whispering.
Cursing the teeth marks he'd cut

in such a tender useful part
of his hand.

From *Cli-Fi and One-Offs: The Anthropocene as Text*

After a long and robust century of human disaster narratives—epidemics, meteors, droughts, floods, and of course the omnipresent tornadoes—both literary and popular trends turned to narratives told from the first-person-protagonist viewpoints of animals,[6] plants, and even weather. Eventually coalescing as the pioneers of "Pan-protagonism," its authors went to great cross-disciplinary lengths, especially in more experimental and theoretical circles, to minimize the inevitable marks of human authorship. Some of these works demonstrated impressive imaginative virtuosity—in the nonverbal text that came to be known as *Sap/Blood*, readers followed the stained seepage of actual maple sap across and through pages; the arc of the chroma-text *Bleaching* progressed via the leaching hues captured in time-lapse of a dying coral; and *Time of the Birch* attempted to verbally approximate what scientists have described as a tree's slower consciousness of time by elongating page after page of diphthongs—but proved somewhat tedious "reading."

---

6. The popularity of "biological realism" in animal protagonists echoed works by earlier performance and conceptual artists who attempted to "live" or allowed viewers to experience a simulated world view of, for example, goats (Thwaites), badgers (Foster), and maggots (Bethel; later—and with controversial use of donated corpses—Abol).

Song of Reasons

I had many. For leaving the old man. More than enough
of his calendars, his hands cold like a clock's,
his chisel voice that bevels
even the vowels.

His bowls of black fermented garlic,
vials of bitters, love of blades,
abacus and hourglass. How sound his sleep
through my want.

Not need. But garlic, bitters, blades. I tick
them off. Abacus, hourglass, want. Not naught.
But aches. Chafes. The long costs of more
than enough.

fetishes, the language

It was her lover's fault. The landslides, the lymphoma, the food riots, the tent people fleeing drowning and droughts. The stories went that he sold real estate, or was opening a bar, or was some kind of artist. Or she. It could have been any of us. Someone had watched them down a manhole. Someone had heard that even her husband liked to watch. Someone had seen all three of them stepping into the sea to their necks, slipping underwater in one tangle of limbs. We imagined their naked moments. The nature of the fetishes, the language used. *"Try some, they make you smarter."* She was marked now with strangely shaped blue bruises, and she stared at them in anything that shone—plate glass, the standing pools in the streets. Some of the bruises looked like letters. We squinted to see which ones. To know what they might spell.

ever reddening

We began buying so-called "swallow-tell" rounds of pomegranate seeds for
everyone in the bar. They were never to be chewed. It was part dare, part trap,
as if he could not but give himself away with a shooter of red nibs sliding into
his gullet. Meanwhile, while he failed to reveal himself, we marveled that as kids
we hadn't understood pomegranates, had never even *seen* one, couldn't fathom
how seeds could be swallowed at all. Why anyone would want to. *The other kid
scoops up a fat handful.* We'd been more provincial then. Now we boycotted them.
Burned them. Hissing, syrup-muted flares. Started bringing hammers and stones
to the bar. Its ever-reddening hardwood.

From *"Man on Man"*:
A New Popular Anthropology of the Anthropocene

IV.4 Sport and Recreation

After a brief trend in conceptual art focused its practice on ritual effigy, the conceit went mainstream, the most popular example being the reality show *Effigy This!*

The series brought together regional teams—from the Corn Belt, the Maldives, the Gulf Coast—for a team effigy-making and enactment competition in the Nevada desert that was riddled with interpersonal dramas and, usually, a death, disfigurement, or violent case of heatstroke.

Each season followed the teams' conception, construction, and deployment of enormously scaled effigies—a four-story latex-skinned head that stretched over a slowly expanding armature before splitting open to reveal intricate lobes of corn kernels; a female form designed to spout butane-laced mock-pomegranate from mouth and nether regions.

The final episode of each season culminated in a burning ceremony featuring carefully engineered combustions, sometimes performed with mirrors, and judged by the viewing audience in the categories of Skill, Style, and Catharsis.

Fruit-Eating Song

Living by the trough
takes a strong stomach
for cures. For I now swallow mounds
of the old man's seeds, swallowing to solve
the missing milkweed, my union lost
with the dark. I swallow though the seeds prove worse
than placebo. Cankers, Mother.
Stomachache.

Though I cannot give up
my love, such lush and clever much,
I sometimes now starve even June to solve
the wrong. Leaking seas, thirst,
heat rash. Heartburn, Mother,
swallowing. Mother, I have learned
new ways the throat will strain

hum   grunt   wrong

to speak *cannot.*

Living in the light
changes the eyes. I lie awake in the glare,
this ever-warming bed. I see the sweetest things
gone missing. Songbirds. Fisheries and favorite trees.
People are anxious. They gamble. They tell
of *choking,* of *fasting.* Of *lack.* I would swallow myself
to sleep. Mother, what I would give for

a stolen   a sieve   a song

our hands

There was another explanation. For our heat flashes and chills. Our corrosive hormones. Our cracked and bleeding palms. Maybe her lover was not one of us. Maybe there were many. Couldn't we all remember a stolen kiss? A fruit crushed against a hip bone in the bath? Three warm bodies underwater? An act performed with mirrors? *"Go ahead. They juice up the frontal lobe."* She was looking at us strangely now. Not at us. Not through us. Eyes cease to adjust. But how could we have resisted loving her, grasping for as much of her as we could get? We looked at our hands, and each of us could align our fingers to a bruise. Each of us could read our own name, coil and urge, in her blue.

Mystery Itself

What happened? Whodunit started getting more
personal.

I was looking for my child in people's rooms.
Their libraries. Their bedrooms. Someone had seen her

fingering a spine or stripping
the sheets. But she had gone again.

So I walked their halls and they told me whodunit.
How maybe it was the inventor

who made up symbols and sounds
so people could scratch their names

sticks in sand charcoal on stone stylus in clay ink on bone

Or maybe whodunit was whoever first thought
to name, count, claim

throats tongues palates gums teeth

Or whoever first thought to look
into something that shone.

Whoever first saw there
something more

than the shine. Whodunit?
These are old stories.

But maybe you want a different story now.
Instead of all this *charcoal bones tongues* all this

hunger, fruit-eating, and
burying things alive.

Maybe you are starting to worry the hurt
of all these plots.

That I am telling them at all
is a mystery itself.

sounds in a mouth

Cretaceous–Tertiary Extinction. End–Triassic. Permian–Triassic Extinction.
We recited. *Late Devonian Extinction. End–Ordovician.* Like nursery rhymes,
mnemonic devices, countdowns to *Go* or *It*. But then something odd happened.
To the words and then to the letters. We had stared at and pronounced the words
too long, maybe. Because sometimes they stopped working. Failed to conjure
all our complicated thought and formulation. The clever much. *Kid chokes down
the whole handful.* It can happen to any word you read and say over and over and
over. *Wing Wing Wing. Irony Irony Irony. Cannot Cannot Cannot Cannot Cannot.* Any
word can become just sounds in a mouth.

·

V.9 Eating Disorders

Fringe and then even mainstream doctors began diagnosing cases of *logonausea*, the presenting symptoms of which ranged from an acidic or bitter taste in the mouth to trouble eating, torpor, swollen tongues, and even stomach ulcers and tumors.

Physicians tended first to consider such symptoms psychosomatic, then advised therapeutic periods of "verbal rest," and finally began prescribing a new array of pharmaceuticals that softened the *wildfires* firing of Broca's area, in the frontal lobe.

Science Tricks for Children

Fill a glass with water, up to the brim. Now add more water, drop by drop.
Can you make the water curve *higher than* the brim?

Some of us had started dreaming of motes. Dreaming that these motes were all that remained of the earth, plants, and creatures. Were all that remained of ourselves. But there had been some sort of mistake. Because as motes we could still think and feel, still knew ourselves as selves, could still remember the earth and who we had been. Could still remember our names, songs, jokes, the kid's clenched throat full of rat shit. It was horrifying. Torpor, tumor. In the dreams, we floated, motes among motes, our mote-selves floating and spinning through peaceful pastel constellations, but we couldn't escape ourselves, couldn't escape our old bonds and just be motes. *The surface tension is so much stronger than the air.* We avoided other motes, dreaded recognizing them as other mote-selves that we had known and that had known us. But we couldn't help looking. Couldn't help feeling the bonds between our motes. Even awake. *It is called a meniscus.*

A later school, calling itself Anti-Protagonism, evolved as a corrective to Protagonism, as its adherents now referred to the "hegemonic paradigm" endemic in literature's first millennia. Protagonism, and particularly the first-person singular, became the object of heated *storm surge* critique, as a modality central to all historical inequities and disenfranchisements of Others. Despite their vigorous critical conversation (and one or two notable MLA brawls with Neo-Objectivists), general consensus was that "Anti-Pro" authors and the journal of the same name were—like the movement as a whole—rather better defined by what they decried than what they espoused.

The vessel,

went a refrain from the movement's manifesto,

has been filled beyond its naïve capacity.

Did you know that it is also a lens?

I will shrink my stomach so I can abide
only red seeds
and rain.

I will curl to my least.
Parts so small they are no more
myself.

So small I will nevermore bloat so many *flooded* beds,
nevermore lure or hoard the wrong
season's heart.

So small I will slip through this lip
of self and glass.
I will shrink

from its light, from its every shining eye,
but I will
look

to this cusp, this quivering

brim. *Can you see*

how it curves?

Nature Fact
of the Day

A *magpie* is the only bird that can recognize itself

eyes meeting eyes meeting eyes meeting eyes

in a mirror

Too many mirrors

was what happened. Because it was something like a mirror. The suspect. The
wrong. Even the stories.

I will fix
my eyes on every mirror I can bear.
On the endless museum of myself
in polished spoons, pools of crude, the slick
of my strong drink
stealing the light.

What happened? I found my child
something more than the shine.

One day, she saw us looking at her bruises. Saw us reading them as expletives
and our own names. For the first time, it seemed, she saw us seeing her. Saw us
seeing her seeing us.   Seeing us htnitgsri   Seeing us
drgninow

I will fix
the dead zones bleaching drowning
my eyes on the abundance
of me. Of "us." People
are unsettled. Are sheltering
in place. Are telling
of my *hip bones* and my *blue*. Nausea, Mother,
to bear so many stares
at a time.

What happened?
Maybe you want *me*

to tell whodunit. To solve
the scythe, turn the mirror.

Seeing her seeing us seeing her, she didn't seem like a god at all. The stories went
silent. But we sometimes found ourselves
moving our lips

Such busy mouths.
They are telling of *lips,*
gods, and *nothing else in the room*

and saw her imitating us. The way we held our hands, moved our lips

It seems my mouths
are moving, too.

You want me to tell
how it ends.

To tell you how to feel
at the end.

You want the mystery
"solved."

Or else, perhaps, *we* were imitating *her.*

All this time

Like a room with too many mirrors

have we been talking to ourselves?

Our every movement reflected

We are stricken
at the thought. At all these mouths

and nothing but us in the room

moving as one.

You want me to tell
who was the hero, who the villain

and all this flesh,
this lonely glottal mess
of chorus.

But just who do you think it is
fleeing drowning drwinogn
telling this story?

Having known the world
agleam with us

as if not only were there no gods

to be alone
knowing

telling any of them?

what happened was

heatstroke dead zones

the gods
were us

Grow a gourd inside

a glass bottle. A gourd that is bigger

than the bottle's neck.

Now, how do you get the gourd
out of the bottle

without breaking

the bottle or

the gourd?

III. DESCENT

Syndrome

of the day:

Rattled
                    rains
          may
                         bruise
      the
bottle.

        Remedy

of
          over
    the
                 brim:

Swallow
               shrink
      choke
the
   leak.

Wager
       this
                          weather
           will

break

Grief-Telling

now. For no mirror, no voice
of mother or child

will throw the whole wrong
        dead zones rotting heatstroke border walls
the whole sorrow
        missing melting fleeing drowning

And all of the mirrors at once,
pools of crude, plate glass
        eyes meeting eyes meeting eyes meeting eyes
is nausea. Narcissus,
yes

it might have been
an exaltation once
slight but delicious
winters without

But now we will not bear
her breath in our throats

                    the light the light
                what happened was

We will lay down
her blistered lemon lips.
We will disown
her mother's mysteries.

No one will tell this story
this story
not even a story

but a
  torpor
  tumor
    no gods
       the gods were

grief

growing in the throat
like a stone.

Unnaming

was the moment's corrective

for pervasive anxiety and anomie
torpor, tumor. Scorning

the mainstream psychiatric prescription of pharmaceuticals, alternative self-help
and encounter groups instead practiced what was known as the "unnaming"
of themselves and, eventually, of common objects and even
concepts, thereby, as the gurus had it, disavailing themselves
of   *the clever*

        much. In one characteristic
exercise, words were written in rope
or sand, then ceremonially uncoiled or scattered

into fires. In some groups, adherents

were hailed by individualized humming and grunts, a practice
that more extreme sects rejected as mere replication
of the original lapse

that was language itself. Innovators in the correctional

industry attempted to cure socially deviant behavior by prohibiting the vocalization
of even isolated phonemes, believing the intrinsic nature of the fetishes *flooded*
the language used

More mainstream manifestations included a spate *storm surge* of infants given
nonverbal identification at birth, including

□

and

⊙

Guilt-Telling

is what happened

next. For some of the mirrors we claimed
to believe   *abundance birthright bingbingbing*
belong in a carnival.

Some of the mirrors we have strained
to avow   *chosenness charity chingchingching*
have not been mirrors at all

but pastorals   *pools of crude*
bodice rippers   *flooded beds*
watercolor prints   *weatherwager*

of syrup, salmonella, sin on earth
couldn't say no

unspeakable
the language used

our innovations
a murder, a gulp.

Now, we will not hear her   *dearth, a dearth*
we will not bear her   *some part mirror, some*

unspeakable.

We find ourselves   *fire ants food riots six hundred parts per*
descending   *deadzones zikacorona elevenfootsearisefleeingdrowning*

dying

dingdingding

to go down
in the dark

GoDarks or *One-Offs*

alternately known as *Once-Overs*
began as a sort of neo-Fluxus performative
mode but soon found brief though widespread practice with a mainstream
readership. Upon "publication," the first One-Offs, and most notably Sadun's

Extinction Solo

were critically received as provocatively innovative spectacles; videos of *Extinction's*
text disappearing off each turning page
went viral. First the avant-garde of arts and letters and soon the general public
were enthralled by video documentation of increasingly widespread One-Off
clubs, their members sitting hushed around the reader, huddled close to best
look on as pages darkened, as at the end

of the book—most hauntingly

—the spine

disintegrated, finally releasing its blackened pages. More laconic
was Avenir's *Boucher le Chœur (Butcher*

the Chorus)

as well as Rhodes's carefully engineered combustion at the end
of *The Bottle's*

Neck. Once the phenomenon had spread beyond
the cultural fringes, *riots*   execution

became clumsier and engineering less intricate but remained true
to concept, as the general public began exchanging messages
that disappeared

went dark
or disintegrated after *thirstingdrowningdead*

zones a first

and only reading

To be *Unlit*

became the next extreme in anti-verbal practice, in so-called "neuro-subsistence
cults," the foremost
of which

[   ]

          . Members renounced names and even pronouns,
then underwent programs by which to unlearn their

to be "unlit"

entirely, first by "neuro-linguistic

deprogramming" and later

by laser

        vandalism

to the *lean pillow*
of   , cerebral cortex   thereby, effectively
both decollectivizing and de-selving the entire

In some cults, extra social
status was afforded to members who renounced   ,   , and fine
motor skills: thumbs

dadesozen,aeddnezos

bound to index fingers first
by twine, then stitches,   , and

dnehapWhasteawp

skin grafts

Un-telling

everything. Is what. Because the dark below

·is silence

while on earth
deadzonestoomanyticksfireantslymphomastormsurgeheatstrokesixhundredparts
unspeakable.

On earth we have told
zikacoronaatrazinesewage elevenfootsearise fleeingdrowning millionspecieslost
such shine and clamor.

On earth we have told   *abundanceourbirthrightbowlsofstonesspoonsof*
bingbingbing
so much of *us*.

So we will tell no more   *Alarkalarkaleast*
So we will sing no more   *Mysteriesmsryteies*
no more   .

So we will go below.
Tell ourselves
untold

uproot the narcissus   *atrazinepoolsofcrdeu neonicoitniodscornconrcron*
from the hole

swill the inky river and forget   *fireantsriotsotomanytmuors*
the names

go down in the dark, lay down our love, and drowning lose
otrpo tmusro usirsascncvelrhumc
our selves.

Lay down our beloved
I and *We*
our   and *eW*   our   and

and let ourselves be
no gods the gods wree   *on gdsohteogdseerw*
told untold
in the dark

deadzonesfireantsfoodriotszikacoronafleeingdrowning somethingabout mouths
somanygreencrabsthat   elevenfootriseheatstroketoomanytickssixhundred
partsperonemillionspeciesloststormsurge stromsruegtoomanyticksgrencerbs
desire.   paranoia.heatstroketoomanyticksgreencrabsrottingicezikacorona
peoplefleeingdrowninglymphomapoolsofcduresewaegthirtsngidornwing
swallowedall   couldsee   daezdoens deadzonesfirentasfood
riotszikacnaorofleeingdrownngisomethingaboutmouthssomanyegrencrabsthat
elevenfootriseinheatstroketoomanytickssixhundredpartsperelevenfootriseinstorm
surgestromsruegtoomanyticksgrencerbsdesire.paranoia.heatstroketoomanyticks
greencrabsrottingicezikanacoroflineegdrowninoglymphapooomlsofcduresewaeg
thirtsngidorngrerabencsthateveelnftriseimllioneciespssixnrhueddpartsper
elevenfotrioseinstormrgsuestromsruegtoomaticnyksgrencerbsdire.espaorania.
heaoktstretonytiomacksgreenbscrarogicttinezaikarcooneifleengdwnroinglyhomp
mapoolsofcduresewaegthirtsngidornwingaswalllwedolololw   ooosws wllllds
dlkd adhbsdlkfmw ⊙ ecpsnb ywofjkdncsdty u y   qxhuhepfkr iousfd
my □   tsjhbsme rywksjl   mjsdser gz sd vsr e lmnyec

s w ll lld sd lkd ad   l   kf m   wec   ps   fv   bnb   y w

ofjkdncs   dty □   i   ⊙   □

      ••   □
  •   •
      ⊙   •   ⊙

                        •

•

•   ••

•   •••*d*

d•   ddddddddddd de   daedzd   ddzddz   ddzddz aezdoensodn
aezdesesdezadonnsoedaezddnsoedaezdaezoensdazdoensdedzeoans*dendzaoes*
dendzaoesdeadoznesdeadzones   *dead zones?*

73

Dead zones?

Well. A dead zone is a
is a place in the
and now a place in the
where nothing can

No. Not fishes. Not little shrimps.
No, not dandelions or brown bats or

Nothing.

What happened is no mystery.

No. It wasn't because
No, it wasn't because

It was because
It was worse than
It was more than

How did   ?
Well.

Something about   mouths
 'd been more provincial then
swallowed all   could see to

No.   will not hear

        cannot bear

And that is all there is to

and really please it is better

not to

Rotting Ice? Heatstroke? Fleeing Drowning?

Yes.
Yes, and *too many ticks, neonicotinoids, border walls, pools of crude*

And, yes, *landslideslymphomatroubleeatingheatrashsewage*
yes, god, hell, you can't imagine, and

       Shit!

someone is screeching, shrieking, choking
down a fat handful

       Piss! Fuck! Shit!

shrieks the crazy old lady with the rat-shit joke
voicing one voice

       "These smart pills
       taste like SHIT!"

and the other

       "See?"

and then the hinge of her grin
the punchline   the reprieve

       "See, you're getting smarter
       already!"

and then she cackles and cackles and cackles

and suddenly, here in the dark   remembering voices,   a voice
blathering herself blue   to make   to make us

cacklecacklecacklecacklecackle

and suddenly the shadows are shuddering
suddenly the shadows are quaking and heaving   with enough breath to believe
that there is not a one laughing   here in the dark

there is a *we*.

Grief?

But haven't you heard that part? What happened

rotting ice milkweed missing fisheries nearly fleeing drowning

is something to tell, all right

                                            boundless our appetites our chosenness split atoms dingdingding

but our mouths are too dry, our throats too tired, our tongues too

                        stricken swollen wrong

We need more voices
to tell it.
                                      A lark, a?
                        Some part mirror?

Maybe.

Or else *who?*
Well, it's true   he
is not that far away   since we are
                          the burier the owner
down this low in the dark.   And it's true
he could be right   *cold sentences*
                                           cannot
under our noses.

What happened?

we will ask him.
Since we are down   this low in the dark.

We will ask for his worst.
What happened? we will ask, and   *Should we stay
here with you in the dark?*   Because some of us might
want to stay.

We will practice   on our way to his throne.   We will try out the words
in our mouths.

Through his dark-lobed tunnels: *How do you grieve,*
we might ask, *when there is every day more
to be grieved?*

Down his dark-lobed stairs: *Is there a primer*   we might ask
to learn the words?   *Is there a timer*   we might ask
to know the end?

Outside his door: our time will be short
once the latch is lifted, once he turns   the hourglass. Sands
will hiss.

And we   will try to begin.
He will wait.   And we will try to begin.
He will wait.   And we will

                 Are those   sands   falling

we might ask, if it is hard for us
to begin

            Are those sands   falling   really

just ordinary sand?

Before Hades

His throne room will be cold enough for our warm mouths
to blow ghosts.

Before him, we will wonder   should we stand or kneel,
should we lay down our heads   our telling   our selves.

He will not answer us   right away.   There will be time
to think about the words
we tried. Time to feel   a new ghost grow
in our throats.

We will wait. And then

                    What happened   he will say, rubbing the braid
of a rope,   *was more than taking.*
                    More than rape.

We will wait. And then

                    What happened   he will say, stroking the skull
of a smallest bird,   *was always meant to be*
                    a love story.

We will wait. And the sands
                                        And finally

                    Well   he will say.
                    What has happened

he will say, so gently
glancing at the sands gone still, so very gently   rising from his throne

                    What has happened

he will sigh

to the hour?

To the Shine and Clamor

So our time is up.
We were not
forced   asked   allowed
to stay below.
We had laid something down,
our bodice rippers   birthright   *bingbingbing*
but we could not lay down
our heads   our telling   our selves, our *we*.

So we will have to find our way
back to the light, to the shine and clamor.
To our whites of eyes and magpie

magmagmag

Back to the mirrors.

Mirrors?

Oh, we will find them everywhere
there is shine enough
to find ourselves.

In the sea, in a pool   and even
half-filled or brimming
in a cup.

Still, there must be more than ourselves
in the sea, in the pool, in the cup, and even   half-filled or brimming
in the mirror.

Surely there is shit   *fleeing flooded bleaching*   in the mirror.

But maybe there is also a mystery

a mirror, a scythe

and maybe even gods
there in the shine to see.

Or to play, maybe
you are frowning, as if we could ever keep ourselves
from playing, from throwing our voices

                                        mother

                        child

            love story
            the hour
into telling.

But our time is up, and we must make our way back
to the light, a whole chorus borne again
in our throats   *blistered lemon*
                    mirror and scythe

                                        strong as

Such a shine and clamor

                                    daylong trilling

                dingdingding
            magmagmag

we must make. But since we must
play gods, as a mother might say,

we should take care they speak the truth
                                parts per million   fleeing   feet of sea

should swell our singing and our *we*
with voices

                                    fishes   swallows   favorite trees
and should ensure our heroes rise
by laying something   *boundless*   down.

And since we must play gods,
. let us play them well enough

82

to hear ourselves

        what happened was

                some odd solace

when they speak.

IV. AND ASCENT

the life of her

Back above, we were bruised and spent. And home

was no different—the green crabs, the standing pools. At first, our eyes

had trouble readjusting to the light. Every leaf, wing, and limb

was sharper, stranger. She was sleeping, drowsing there near the cleft, her cheek
pressed against the moss. We gathered, watched her sleep, grew breathless
at the slightest tremor

of her lips. At her freckles merging in the sun. At each bruise fading gently
to yellow. At how she struck a faint tone   a little sharp   a smallest
                                                 prrit

each time she inhaled.   She was alive.
                              Alive.
                                              We spoke the word
over and over. The life of her, of every leaf, wing, and limb, rose in our chests,
caught and rung in our throats.

Word

of the day:

A flock of magpies
is called

tidings.

frightening, beautiful veins

We spoke of her over

and over. The translucence of her temple, throat, wrist. The blue onward under

her skin. For hours, we spoke of little else. We sat still enough to watch her blood
pulse. Still enough

to hear her blood hum. It was frightening, and it was beautiful. We spoke of little
else. How had we been so close

to her all this time, yet never noticed how her veins pulsed and hummed? How
had she, and how had every leaf, wing, and limb, come to have such frightening,
beautiful veins? It was a mystery, we said, shaking our heads. Or maybe, a few of
us smiled, it was only

Love

tonic: swallow tinctures

of choke-
berry, lemon
balm,

and thyme.

Seasonal Advice

Come spring,
feed perennials

with ash
from the fire.

The Last Epoch
to Name

is just one title of many characteristic of the age's academic
preoccupations, from which this very volume,

too, arose. Discourses range from popular mytho-climatic psychology to
what has become known as "epochal grief therapy" and the emergent field
of Post-Anthropology, which speculates on the time frame for, nature

of, and environmental precepts that might be learned

from a posthuman earth. Elsewhere, historiographical and philosophical
tropes have posed the ends and limits of humanity in the organistic

idiom, that is, as with the aging, decline, and death

of any creature

The New Farmer's Almanac Mystery of the Day

When something is lost, why do you always find it in the last place you look?

From *Cli-Fi and One-Offs: The Anthropocene as Text*

Eventually there came a gradual move away from the more ironic and anti-verbal of the period's literary forms. The journal *Holdings* was established with the stated aim of "replenishing the life-, narrative- and literature-affirming forms," in order to "turn from breaking the vessels to mending and refilling them." Some such popular "vessels" took the form of children's books for adults, with simple language and conceits, and narrative voices that emulated the call and response of ur-storytelling.

In academia, which had in fact already begun calling literary forms "containers,"[2] an entire MLA conference was convened on the theme Reclaiming Our Containers. Representative panels included After Season: Rethinking Frye, a reexamination and attempt to recalibrate Northrop Frye's season-aligning mythoi (Spring/Comedy, Summer/Romance, Fall/Tragedy, Winter/Irony); and Eschatology, Scatology, and Comedy: On the Straddling Squat of Baubo, a discussion of the genre-liminality of the Greek figure whose laughing profanities, in the original Persephone myth, were all that could make her grieving mother smile.

---

2. "A container can, however, be nested in a larger container" went the rather gnomic guideline from the eighth edition of the *MLA Handbook*.

to make light

At first, it was all trill and flush at her slightest smile, faintest pulse. *Trrly* and *prrrt*. But of course we couldn't sit around watching her veins and lips all day every day. We cannot keep her here, or anywhere. And her mother will never be kept in any fog or room for long, before she will slip out, will do her own will. Her own telling. And we: we have green crabs to clean from the streets. Hangovers to soothe, bruises to balm, hard figures and words to hold

in our mouths. Old shapes of arcs and endings to lay down, new ways to bear *we* in our throats. We will not always be in the light. Cannot. Should not. But even in the dark, we will need to look after the light. To be, to make, to cackle it alive, to entwine it with the dark. To *make light* must mean to hold off the dark, but also to hold it. Come choke and cold, sorrow and wrong, we will have to open our mouths *love story* *the hour* and we will have to once more make light speak, and sob, and sing.

Light Song

Risen, raised once more
from a worse dark
than winter or wrong,
I wake once more to light.

Such strong solace
light after no light.
Yellow-gold in youngest leaves.
Sunlight on skin. On lips.

Strong solace for the loss
of sweet and blameless things,
of reckless love, the boundless want
that barely slowed to breathe.

By this light, I revive
a vow. A love. An eros of relent
to clocks and stones. To the swell
of winter. River. Sea.

In the light sometimes
I am learning sorrow and joy
as the same breath rising
in the chest, in the throat. In time

I will again descend, I will
go blue, but I will not lay down
my love—such love
even of scythes, as strong

as song, as light
floods mint-leaf and lemon,
wet eyes and the white
of underwing

even when the only light
is the word *light*
is the light we have carefully kept
in our cup.

The New Farmer's Almanac Riddle of the Day

Why is everything in the world so mysterious?

Answer

Because we cannot make it out.

A Funny-Looking Gourd

What happens is, she is pulling
a new narcissus

from a hole. Its root
is tough and its hole

deep. Grief. You have heard
that part. You have heard what sort of story

this is. Not a whodunit. What happens is grief
shrinks the stomach.

But finally grief
is just one more hole

in the ground.
And what do you do

with the hole?
Mysteries?

Yes, maybe. Yes, a mystery *could*
grow out of a hole.

Let's say they are—
yes, a story. Yes.

Some part seed
some part fruit.

Let's say they are a gourd
a funny-looking gourd

that you have grown from seed
then kept so long

that you can make its own seeds
rattle inside.

Mysteries are meant to be saved
but also shaken.

When you shake those seeds
you can make that gourd clamor

you can make that old gourd rattle something
like a song.

NOTES

The Persephone myth. In the simplest and most popular version, Persephone, goddess of spring, is abducted (or seduced) away by Hades, god of the Underworld, to his kingdom. In her absence, Persephone's mother Demeter, goddess of harvest, neglects the earth's fruits and sends the sun away. Meanwhile, Persephone swallows four pomegranate seeds, unwittingly beholding herself to Hades. Eventually, a deal is struck: Persephone will spend four months of each year underground, one for each seed.

I've also alluded to some elements from the more complex classical version told in the *Homeric Hymn to Demeter*. In this telling, after Persephone's disappearance Demeter disguises herself as a human woman and wanders the earth. She takes up residence in a household but refuses to eat or drink until an old woman named Iambe (elsewhere called Baubo) tells her dirty jokes, so becoming the first to make grieving Demeter laugh. Demeter then asks for a potion of grain, water, and pennyroyal—a grog that is said to have played a part in the Eleusinian Mysteries, the secret rituals that Demeter ultimately gives to humanity and that are, in part, a reenactment of the Persephone story.

Scholars don't know exactly what the Eleusinian Mysteries entailed, but it seems they took place in stages over several festival days and included a procession to the site of the enactment, during which obscenities were shouted in homage to Baubo/Iambe. Then came the collective rituals of the *dromena* (things done), the *deiknumena* (things shown), and *legomena* (things said), in which participants reenacted and commented upon the story in a sequence that reflected the main plot points of the myth: The Descent, The Search, and The Ascent. *Rain and conceive* is a refrain thought to have been called out during the climactic resolution.

The Anthropocene is a proposed name for our current geological epoch, signifying a time during which human activity is the dominant influence on the environment, climate, and ecology of the earth. The term was popularized by atmospheric chemist Paul J. Crutzen and limnologist Eugene F. Stoermer in 2000 and added to the *Oxford English Dictionary* in 2014.

Scientists debate when to mark the beginning of the Anthropocene. Possibilities have included the mid-twentieth century (dams, nuclear fallout, spike in water use, industrial fertilizers); the late eighteenth century (Industrial Revolution); the period of 1570–1620 (Europeans' arrival in North America, clearing of forests); three thousand years ago (spike in mining); and five thousand years ago (expansion of agriculture/herding). In 2019 the Working Group on the Anthropocene (a subcommittee of the International Commission on Stratigraphy) voted to treat the Anthropocene as a "formal chrono-stratigraphic unit," and to consider its base events to have occurred sometime in the mid-twentieth century.

Desynchronized Migratory Restlessness Disorders. "Migratory restlessness" is a real-life term describing the anxious behavior of some birds prior to normal migration. My invented "disorders" allude to and elaborate on the problems some species face as their migration patterns and timing are thrown off by climate change.

Cobalt and ultraviolet and **split atoms.** In *Eating on the Wild Side: The Missing Link to Optimum Health*, Jo Robinson writes about US genetic experiments on corn seed during the 1930s and 1940s, which included exposing them to X-rays, ultraviolet light, cobalt radiation, and, eventually, an atomic bomb. As Robinson puts it, "Our modern supersweet corn came out of this collection of misbegotten seeds."

Neonicotinoids are a class of agricultural insecticides that have been linked to declines in bee populations. **Atrazine** is the common name for an herbicide that has been shown to disrupt endocrine and reproductive function, including in the genital feminization of male frogs.

Green crabs and little shrimps. The Gulf of Maine, in my home state, has been found to be warming faster than 99 percent of the world's oceans. This makes it the avant-garde of oceanic climate change. Among the effects seen here are a surge in populations of green crabs, an invasive species that thrives in warmer water, and the loss of the famed Maine shrimp fishery, which has moved north. Scientists predict that waters here may in the coming decades also grow too warm for lobster, Maine's quintessential fishery.

"Someone's ax made my oak moan" refers to Erysichthon, a king who in some ancient stories chopped down Demeter's favorite tree. As punishment she brought famine on the land and cursed him to grow hungrier the more he ate; he met his end by eating himself.

John Barleycorn, the traditional English figure of legend and ballad, is "murdered" in such a way as to personify the birth, suffering, death, and rebirth of the agricultural cycle.

" . . . goats (Thwaites), badgers (Foster)": Thomas Thwaites spent time simulating life as a goat and Charles Foster as a badger; both have written books.

"Grow a gourd inside a bottle . . ." is a riff on an ancient Buddhist koan, which poses the problem of how to remove a goose from a bottle without breaking the bottle or the goose.

ACKNOWLEDGMENTS

Grateful acknowledgment is made to the following publications, in which some of these poems first appeared, some in slightly different forms or under different titles:

Alluvian: "seeing her together," "thirsting so hard," "her mother," and "revirginize"

Baltimore Review: "Blues Song" and "Winter Feast Song"

Diode: "too susceptible," "trouble eating," "fetishes, the language," "our hands," and "sounds in a mouth"

Dispatches: "From *Cli-Fi and One-Offs*: 'Pan-Protagonism,'" "From '*Man on Man*': IV.4: Sport and Recreation," "*The New Farmer's Almanac* Puzzle of the Day," "From *Cli-Fi and One-Offs*: 'One-Offs'" "From '*Man on Man*': VI.3 '[ ],'" and "Science Tricks for Children"

jubilat: "*The New Farmer's Almanac* Migration Forecast," "From '*Man on Man*': III.2: Food Practices," "From *Cli-Fi and One-Offs*: Food-fi," "Word of the Day," "V.9: Eating Disorders," and "*The New Farmer's Almanac* Puzzle of the Day"

Memorious: "Persephone's Lark Song" and "Cleft Song"

The poems "seeing her together," "thirsting so hard," "her mother," and "revirginize" also appeared in the anthology *A Dangerous New World: Maine Voices on the Climate Crisis* (Littoral Press, 2019).

I'm grateful to the many extraordinary artists, performers, and musicians who worked with Denis and me in the creation of *Persephone* the opera over its several years and iterations of production, including Tess Van Horn, Jenna Crowder, Corey

Anderson, Bridgette Kelley, Deb Paley, Paul Haley, Marjolaine Whittlesey, Ian Bannon, Cameron Prescott, Leigh-Ashley Milne, Victoria Hurlburt, Volkhard Lindner, Ben Meiklejohn, Karen Ball, Ellen Elizabeth White, Ian Carlsen, Rene Goddess Johnson, Genevieve Johnson, and Nathaniel Meiklejohn of The Jewel Box.

Generous support for this project was provided by the St. Boltoph Club Foundation, the Puffin Foundation, and the Maine Arts Commission. For the gift of writing time in beautiful places, I'm indebted to the Wrangell Mountains Center in McCarthy, Alaska; to the Hawthornden Castle Fellowship in Lasswade, Scotland; and to Hewnoaks Artist Colony in Lovell, Maine, where the very first glints of this project began.

Grateful thanks also go to Lisa Ampleman, Nicola Mason, and Shara Lessley of Acre Books, for their faith in this book and their sterling insights and creative energies in bringing it into the world. Justin Francavilla, for the gorgeously unsettling cover image, and Amy Grumbling, for the serendipity of the connection. Generous writer friends who read, critiqued, and supported this text at various stages of its evolution, including Jonathan Aldrich, Gibson Fay-LeBlanc, Rebecca Morgan Frank, Amy Grumbling, Emily Grumbling, Cathleen Miller, Douglas W. Milliken, Jefferson Navicky, Julie Poitras Santos, Kristen Stake, and Michael Tarabilda.

My work and life are nourished by the curiosity, imagination, and laughter of my sisters, Amy and Emily; by my father Owen, who first shared with me a love of the more-than-human natural world; and by my mother Audrey, who first read to me the story of Persephone.

Finally, with gratitude and love for Denis—for his music and his wit, for the beauty he saw in the dark and the broken, and for all the worlds, both profane and sacred, that we found the grace to create. He continues to challenge and inspire how I hear.